Richard Morse Hodge

Historical Atlas and Chronology of the Life of Jesus Christ

A text book and companion to a harmony of the gospels

Richard Morse Hodge

Historical Atlas and Chronology of the Life of Jesus Christ
A text book and companion to a harmony of the gospels

ISBN/EAN: 9783337164447

Printed in Europe, USA, Canada, Australia, Japan

Cover: Foto ©Lupo / pixelio.de

More available books at **www.hansebooks.com**

THE LIFE OF JESUS CHRIST

A SYLLABUS, TRACING THE DEVELOPMENT OF OUR LORD'S MINISTRY

BY THE REV.

RICHARD M. HODGE, M. A.

Instructor in the Bible Institute, Nashville, Tenn.

1899.

TABLE OF THE GOSPELS ACCORDING TO THE GENERAL DIVISIONS OF CHRIST'S LIFE.

THE MINISTRY OF JESUS CHRIST

L—JESUS' METHOD OF WORK.

Successive Cycles of 1st, Organization ; 2nd, Miracles ; 3rd, Acceptance and Opposition ; 4th, Teaching.

II.—ORGANIZATION AND TEACHING, WITH DATES

PERIOD I—*A. D. 27, January to April.*

ORGANIZATION. Several men beginning to follow Jesus.
GREAT DISCOURSE. With Nicodemus, on the New Birth and Salvation.

PERIOD II,—*A. D. 27, April to December.*

ORGANIZATION. Some disciples baptising under Jesus.
GREAT DISCOURSE. With a Samaritan woman, on Living Water and his Mission.

PERIOD III.—*A. D. 27, December to A. D. 28, April.*

ORGANIZATION. Jesus' disciples leaving business for him.
GREAT DISCOURSE. The Sermon on the Mount, on the Messianic Kingdom.

PERIOD IV.—*A. D. 28, Summer and Fall.*

ORGANIZATION. The Twelve Apostles selected.
GREAT DISCOURSE. First group of parables on the Kingdom of Heaven.

PERIOD V.—*A. D. 28, Fall to A. D. 29, April.*

ORGANIZATION. Apostles sent out two by two on a mission.
GREAT DISCOURSE. On Spiritual Food.

PERIOD VI.—*A. D. 29, April to October.*

ORGANIZATION. Apostles' formal acceptance of Jesus as their Saviour.
GREAT DISCOURSE. On Greatness.

PERIOD VII. - *A. D. 29, October to A. D. 30, January.*

ORGANIZATION. Seventy more disciples sent out on a mission.
GREAT DISCOURSE. Second great group or parables on the Kingdom of Heaven.

PERIOD VIII.—*A. D. 30. January to April.*

ORGANIZATION. The resignation of the apostles to martyrdom.
GREAT DISCOURSES. Great Debate with the Sanhedrists.
Farewell to the Apostles.

PERIOD IX.—*A. D. 30, April 9 to May 18,*

ORGANIZATION. Disciples commissioned to evangelize the world.
GREAT DISCOURSE. On Salvation and the World-Wide Consummation of the Messianic
Kingdom.

III.—MIRACLES IN ORDER

PERIOD I.	PERIOD IV.	PERIOD VI.	PERIOD VIII.
Water into wine.	Centurion's servant.	Demoniac girl.	Lazarus.
	Widow's son.	Deaf man.	Ten lepers.
	Demoniac.	Feeding 4,000.	Bartimaeus and blind
PERIOD III.	PERIOD V.	Blind man.	companion.
Nobleman's son.	Stilling storm.	Transfiguration.	Barren fig-tree.
Draught of fish.	Two demoniacs.	Demoniac boy.	Malchus' ear.
Demoniac.	Woman with flux.	Coin in fish.	
Peter's mother.	Jairus' daughter.		
Leper.	Two blind men.	PERIOD VII.	PERIOD IX.
Paralytic.	Dumb demoniac.	Blind man.	Resurrection.
Infirm man.	Feeding 5,000	Paralytic woman.	Draught of fish.
Withered hand.	Walking on sea.	Dropsical man.	Ascension.

IV.—THE HOSTILITY OF THE RULERS

(1) THE CHALLENGES MADE OF JESUS FOR A SIGN OF HIS CHRISTHOOD.

1. By the Sanhedrists, Jerusalem, met by the "temple sign." (Period I.)
2. By the Pharisees, Capernaum, met by the "Jonah sign." (Period IV.)
3. By Pharisees and Sadducees, Magadan, met by the "Jonah sign." (Period VI.)
4. By the Sanhedrists, Jerusalem, answered by an explicit affirmation of his divinity. (Period VII.)
5. By the Sanhedrists, Jerusalem, met by counter-challenges regarding John the Baptist and the divinity of the Christ. (Period VIII.)

(2) THE CHARGES PREFERRED AGAINST JESUS.

Blasphemy (8).	Mental abberation (3).	Ceremonial uncleanness (2).
Sabbath-breaking (6).	Not fasting (2).	Treason (1).
Low association (5).	Satanic agency (2).	*Total Charges* (29).

(3) HOSTILE QUESTIONS ADDRESSED TO JESUS.

1. By the Pharisees, regarding the punishment of adultery. (Period VII.)
2. By the Pharisees, regarding their own blindness. (Period VII.)
3. By a lawyer, regarding eternal life. (Period VII.)
4. By the Pharisees, regarding the time of the Kingdom. (Period VIII.)
5. By the Pharisees and Herodians, regarding tribute. (Period VIII.)
6. By the Sadducees. regarding resurrection. (Period VIII.)
7. By the Pharisees, regarding the great commandment. (Period VIII.)

(4) THE CONSPIRACY AGAINST JESUS' LIFE.

1. PHARISEES, Jerusalem, inducing Jesus to leave the capital. (Period III.)
2. PHARISEES AND HERODIANS, Capernaum, preventing Jesus' attending the following Passover, or remaining in Galilee after that time. (Period III.)
3. PHARISEES, HERODIANS AND SADDUCEES, Magadan, thwarting Jesus' attempt to re-enter Galilee. (Period VI.)
4. SANHEDRISTS, Jerusalem, compelling Jesus' withdrawal from the capital. (Period VII.)
5. SANHEDRIN, Jerusalem, inducing Jesus' flight from Bethany. (Period VIII.)
6. SANHEDRIN, JUDAS, THE PEOPLE AND PILATE, Jerusalem, securing Jesus' death. (Period VIII.)

V.—JOURNEYS WITH EVENTS IN ORDER AND LOCATION

PERIOD I.

1. BETHANY (Perea), *Baptism*.
2. MT. NEBO, Temptation.
3. BETHANY (Perea), *Disciples met*.
4. CANA, **a** wedding.
5. CAPERNAUM, a visit.
6. JERUSALEM, Cleansing Temple, *Discourse with Nicodemus*.

PERIOD II.

1. JUDEA, *Baptizing*.
2. SYCHAR, *Discourse with woman*, preaching.

PERIOD III.

1. CANA, **N**obleman's son.
2. NAZARETH, Jesus' life attempted.
3. CAPERNAUM, *Disciples called* **from** *business*, demoniac, Peter's **mother**.
4. GALILEE, a leper healed (**First Tour**).
5. CAPERNAUM, Paralytic (**thru** roof).
6. JERUSALEM, Paralytic (**Bethesda**).
7. JUDEA, Plucking corn.
8. CAPERNAUM, Withered hand.
9. MT. BEATITUDES, "**Sermon** *on the Mount.*"

PERIOD IV.

1. MT. BEATITUDES, *Apostles* **selected**.
2. CAPERNAUM, Centurion's **servant**.
3. NAIN, Widow's son **raised**.
4. GALILEE, Inquiry of John Baptist.
5. GALILEE, Sinful woman (Second Tour).
6. **CAPERNAUM**, Demoniac, *Parables*.

PERIOD V.

1. LAKE GALILEE, Storm stilled.
2. GERASA, Demoniacs, swine.
3. CAPERNAUM, Woman, Jairus' daughter, two blind men, dumb demoniac.
4. NAZARETH, Again rejected.
5. GALILEE, *Sending out Apostles* (**Third Tour**).
6. CAPERNAUM, **News of John the** Baptist's death.
7. BETHSAIDA JULIAS, 5,000 **fed**.
8. LAKE GALILEE, Walking **on** water.
9. GENNESARET, Miracles.
10. CAPERNAUM, *Discourse on Spiritual Food*.

PERIOD VI.

1. CAPERNAUM, *Apostles'* **confession**.
2. PHOENICIA, Demoniac **girl**.
3. DECAPOLIS, Deaf man, 4,000 fed.
4. MAGADAN, Met by Sadducees.
5. BETHSAIDA JULIAS, **Blind man**.
6. CAESAREA PHILIPPI, *Apostles' confession*.
7. MT. HERMON, Transfiguration, demoniac.
8. CAPERNAUM, Coin, *Discourse on Greatness*.

PERIOD VII.

1. CAPERNAUM, *The Seventy sent out*.
2. SAMARIA, Inhospitality of a village.
3. JERUSALEM, Hostility of Sanhedrists, blind man healed.
4. JUDEA, Return of the Seventy.
5. JUDEA, a lawyer's question.
6. BETHANY (Judea), Supper.
7. JUDEA, Paralytic woman healed.
8. JERUSALEM, Second stoning for Jesus.
9. PEREA, Dropsical man, *Parables*.

PERIOD VIII.

1. **PEREA**, *Loyalty of Apostles*.
2. BETHANY (Judea), Lazarus raised.
3. EPHRAIM, In retreat from Sanhedrin.
4. SAMARIA, Ten lepers healed.
5. GALILEE, Question on Kingdom.
6. PEREA, Question on divorce, blessing children, rich ruler, ambition of James **and** John.
7. JERICHO, Bartimaeus, Zachaeus.
8. BETHANY (Judea), Supper.
9. JERUSELEM, Entry, cleansing Temple, *Debate with rulers*, Lord's Supper, *Farewell Discourse* **to** *Apostles*, arrest, trials, death, burial of Jesus.

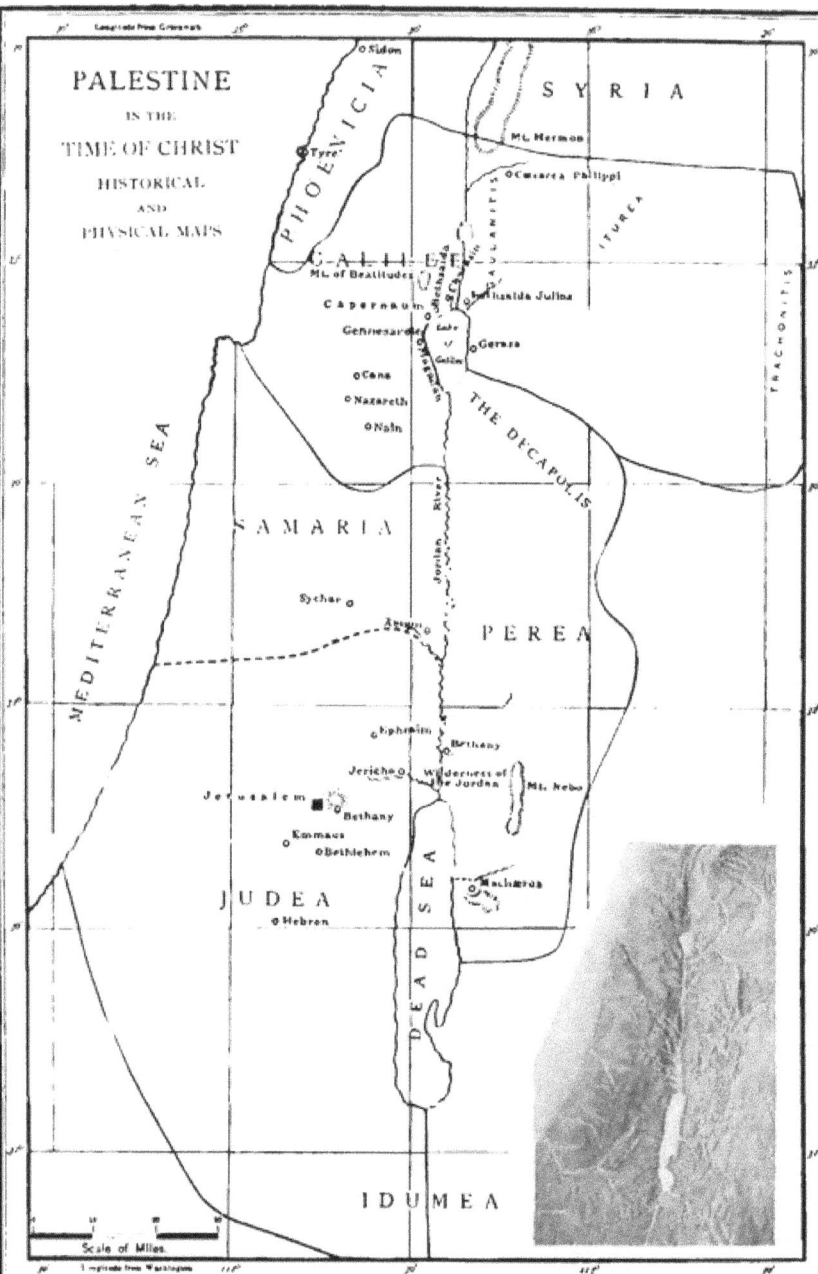

PALESTINE
IN THE
TIME OF CHRIST
HISTORICAL
AND
PHYSICAL MAPS

PHOENICIA

SYRIA

Sidon

Tyre

Mt. Hermon

Caesarea Philippi

ITUREA

GALILEE

Mt. of Beatitudes

Capernaum

Gennesareth

Bethsaida Julias

TRACHONITIS

Lake

Cana

Nazareth

Gerasa

Nain

MEDITERRANEAN SEA

SAMARIA

THE DECAPOLIS

Sychar

Jordan River

PEREA

Ephraim

Bethany

Jericho

Wilderness of the Jordan

Mt. Nebo

Jerusalem

Bethany

Emmaus

Bethlehem

DEAD SEA

Machaerus

JUDEA

Hebron

IDUMEA

Scale of Miles.

HISTORICAL ATLAS AND CHRONOLOGY

OF THE LIFE OF JESUS CHRIST

A TEXT BOOK
AND COMPANION TO A HARMONY OF THE GOSPELS

BY THE REV.

RICHARD M. HODGE, M. A.

Superintendent of the Bible Institute, Nashville, Tennessee

D. A. ST. CLAIR PRESS
WYTHEVILLE, VA.
1899

PREFATORY NOTE

THESE pages contain three exhibits of the life of Christ which have been developed in the class-room in the effort to teach our Lord's life as a history. The historical maps locate in order the principal events of Jesus' life, and are designed for memory pictures. Every map exhibits a different journey and each event is recorded as near its proper place as can be determined. Only the towns, provinces, streams and mountains that are directly involved in the history of Jesus' life are represented. For typographical convenience the "Mount of Beatitudes" is placed a little to the north of the spot generally favored. The chronological table gives all of the reasonably certain years, seasons, months, days, and hours of Jesus' life, and supplements the maps in geographical detail. The third exhibit proposes an analysis of Jesus' ministry based upon his method of work, by recognizing periods, indicated by Jesus himself in the successive stages by which he organized his disciples, and which he invariably punctuated with one of his great discourses. Analyses are given which show the character of each period, and trace the developments, crises and consummations that unfold the plans and purpose of his ministry. The book is best used with a Harmony of the gospels. It will accompany any of the standard works, by Broadus, Stevens and Burton, Riddle, or Robinson, and will not be found to vary from the order of events followed by any of these editors excepting in the few and generally unimportant particulars where they vary from each other. The table of passages according to the general divisions of the life of Christ adopted in this work will serve to locate events in an ordinary version of the gospels.

TABLE OF THE GOSPELS ACCORDING TO THE GENERAL DIVISIONS OF THE LIFE OF JESUS CHRIST ADOPTED IN THIS WORK

CHILDHOOD AND YOUTH OF JESUS
Matthew 1:1-3:12. Mark 1:1-8. Luke 1:1-3:18. John 1:1-18.

MINISTRY OF JESUS CHRIST

PERIOD I
Matthew 3:13-4:11. Mark 1:9-13. Luke 3:21-4:13. John 1:19-3:22.

PERIOD II
Matthew 4:12. Mark 1:14. Luke 4:14. John 3:22-4:43.

PERIOD III
Matthew 4:13-7:29; 8:2-4, 14-17; 9:2-9; 12:1-21. Mark 1:14-2:14, 23-3:19. Luke 4:14-5:28; 6:1-49. John 4:44-5:47.

PERIOD IV
Matthew 8:1, 5-13; 11:2-30; 12:22-13:53. Mark 3:13-4:34. Luke 6:13-16; 7:1-8:21.

PERIOD V
Matthew 8:18, 23-9:1, 10-11:1; 13:54-14:36. Mark 2:15-22; 4:35-6:56. Luke 5:29-39; 8:22-9:17. John 6:1-66.

PERIOD VI
Matthew 15:1-18:35;· 8:19-22. Mark 7:1-9:50. Luke 9:18-50, 57-62. John 6:67-7:9.

PERIOD VII
Luke 9:51-56; 10:1-17:10. John 7:10-10:42.

PERIOD VIII
Matthew 19:1-27:66. Mark 10:1-15:47. Luke 17:11-23:56. John 11:1-19:42.

PERIOD IX
Matthew 28:1-20. Mark 16:1-20. Luke 24:1-53. John 20:1-21:25. Acts 1:3-12. 1 Corinthians 15:5-7.

CONTENTS

HISTORICAL MAPS

NOTES ON MAPS

THE MINISTRY OF JESUS CHRIST

CHRONOLOGY

NOTE ON MAP I

CHRONOLOGY

A stay of probably about two months in Egypt is to be reckoned between Jesus' leaving Bethlehem and his going to Nazareth.

ROMAN RULERS

Herod the Great ruled all Palestine until B. C. 4.

Herod Archelaus ruled Judea and Samaria, B. C. 4 to A. D. 6.

Herod Antipas ruled Galilee and Perea, and Herod Philip his tetrarchy, from B. C. 4 until after the ascension of Christ.

4

PALESTINE
MAP 1
CHRONOLOGY OF
CHRIST'S LIFE
B. C. 5-A. D. 30

ROMAN RULERS
A. D. 26-30

RACES

Longitude from Greenwich

PHOENICIA
GENTILES
A FEW DAYS OR WEEKS

Sidon

Tyre

SYRIA
GENTILES

Mt. Hermon

Caesarea Philippi

GALILEE
JEWS
BALANCE OF SIX MONTHS

Mt. of Beatitudes

Capernaum
Gennesaret
5. SIXTEEN MONTHS
Bethsaida Julias
GENTILES

Gerasa

TETRARCHY OF HEROD PHILIP

Cana

Nazareth
2. THIRTY YEARS

Nain

THE DECAPOLIS
Free Cities
GENTILES

Jordan River

HEROD
ANTIPAS

MEDITERRANEAN SEA

SAMARIA
MIXED RACE

4. A FEW DAYS
Sychar

PEREA
JEWS

PROVINCE OF PILATE

Ephraim
Bethany
8. SIX MONTHS

Jericho
Wilderness of
the Jordan

Mt. Nebo

3. ONE YEAR
Jerusalem

Bethany

Emmaus
Bethlehem

1. TWO MONTHS

JUDEA
JEWS
Hebron

DEAD SEA

Machaerus

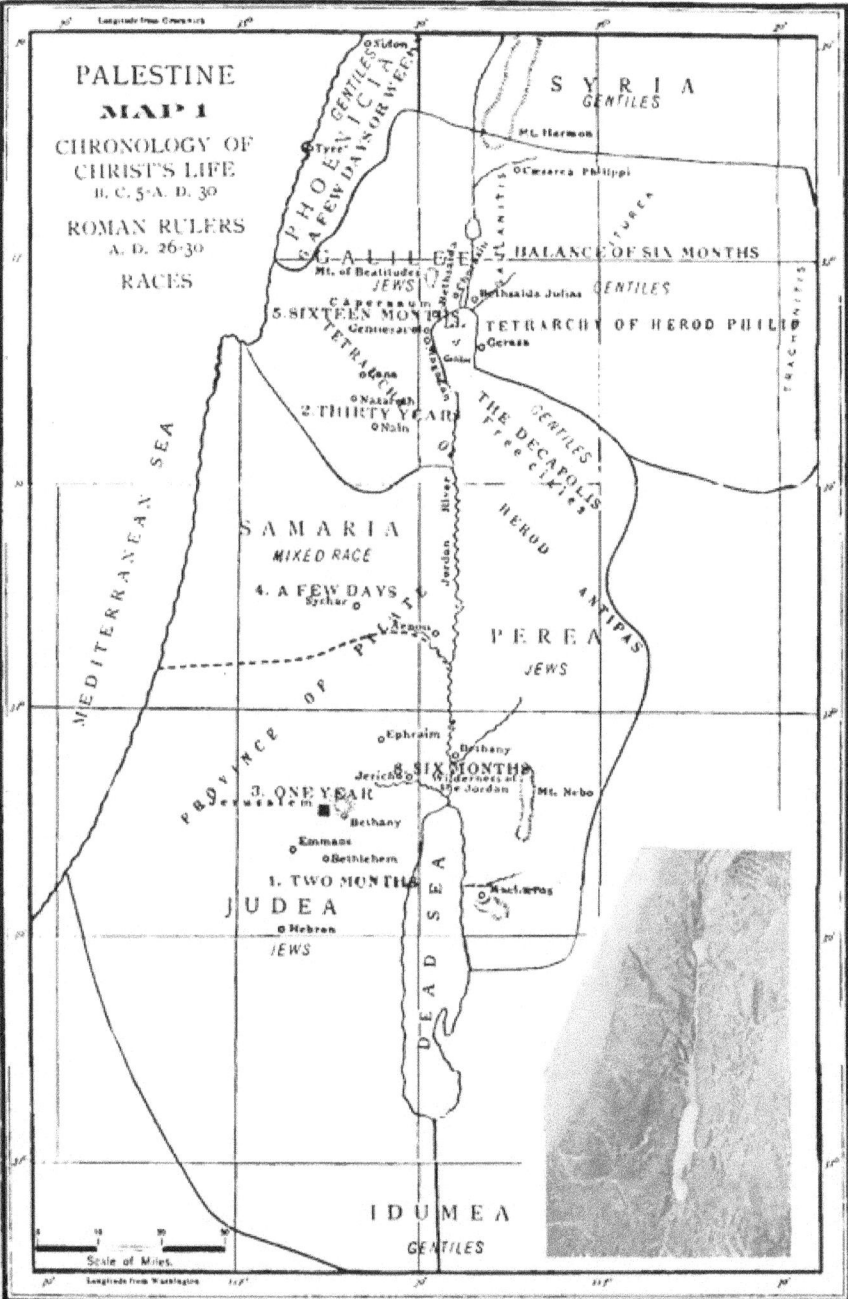

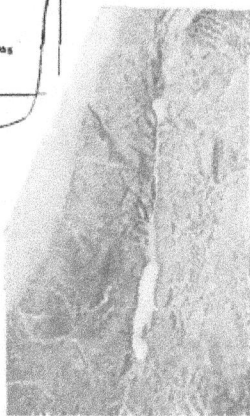

Scale of Miles.

Longitude from Washington

IDUMEA
GENTILES

NOTE ON MAP 2

Hebron is conjectured to be the residence of the parents of John the Baptist, as it was a priest city and the place of most importance in "the hill country of Judea." See Luke 1:65.

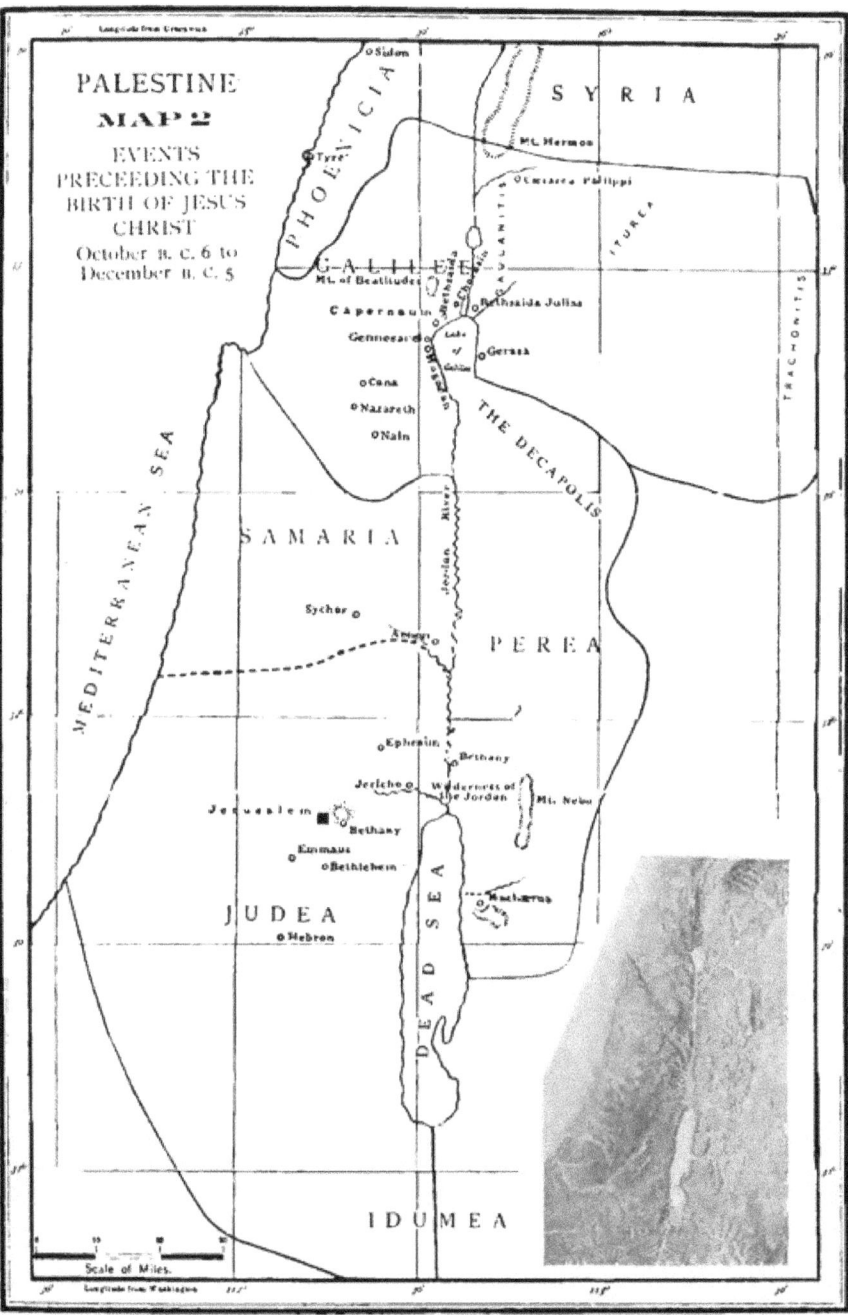

PALESTINE
MAP 2

EVENTS
PRECEEDING THE
BIRTH OF JESUS
CHRIST
October B. C. 6 to
December B. C. 5

SYRIA

PHOENICIA

o Sidon

o Tyre

Mt. Hermon

o Cæsarea Philippi

GALILEE

Mt. of Beatitudes

Capernaum

Gennesaret

Bethsaida Julias

Lake of Galilee

o Gerash

ITUREA

TRACHONITIS

o Cana

o Nazareth

o Nain

THE DECAPOLIS

MEDITERRANEAN SEA

SAMARIA

Sychar o

Aenon o

Jordan River

PEREA

o Ephraim

o Bethany

Jericho o

Wilderness of the Jordan

Mt. Nebo

Jerusalem

Bethany

Emmaus

o Bethlehem

JUDEA

o Hebron

DEAD SEA

o Machærus

IDUMEA

Scale of Miles.

Herod the Great died within less than two months of his slaying the infants of Bethlehem.

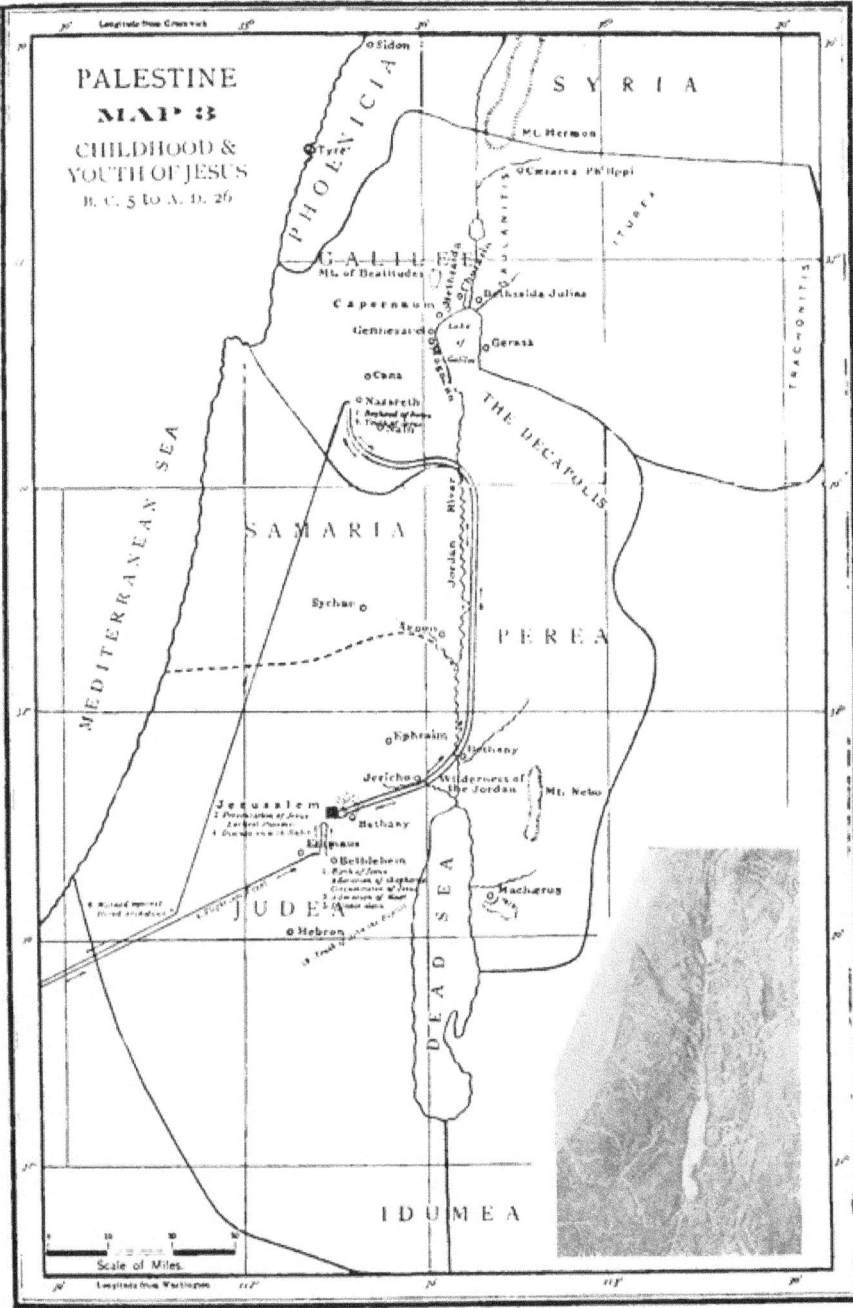

PALESTINE
MAP 3
CHILDHOOD &
YOUTH OF JESUS
B. C. 5 to A. D. 26

John the Baptist's active ministry covered about eighteen months, about one half of which was spent in the Wilderness of the Jordan and at Bethany, and the balance at Aenon. His imprisonment was of fifteen months' duration.

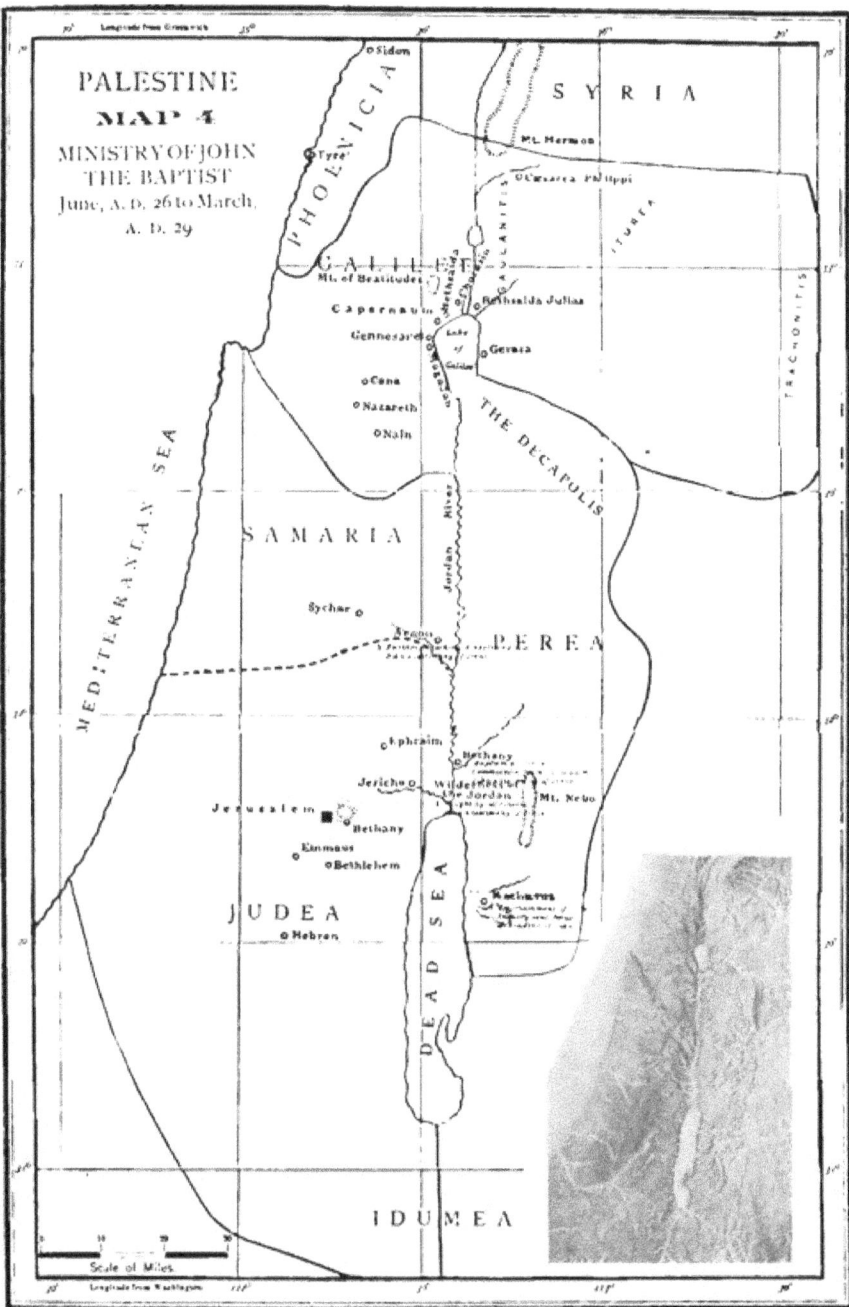

PALESTINE
MAP 4
MINISTRY OF JOHN
THE BAPTIST
June, A. D. 26 to March,
A. D. 29

SYRIA

PHOENICIA

o Sidon

o Tyre

Mt. Hermon

GALILEE

o Caesarea Philippi

GAULANITIS

ITUREA

TRACHONITIS

Mt. of Beatitudes

Capernaum o

Bethsaida Julias

Gennesaret o

Lake of Galilee

Gerasa

o Cana

o Nazareth

o Nain

Jordan River

THE DECAPOLIS

MEDITERRANEAN SEA

SAMARIA

Sychar o

PEREA

Ephraim o

Bethany

Jericho o

Wilderness

Jerusalem

Bethany

Emmaus o

o Bethlehem

DEAD SEA

Mt. Nebo

JUDEA

o Hebron

Machaerus

IDUMEA

Scale of Miles

THE MINISTRY OF JESUS CHRIST

Jesus' ministry is divided into nine periods, according to the several successive steps that he employed in organizing his disciples. Each of the nine periods that result is found also to close with one of Jesus' principal discourses.

ANALYSIS OF THE WORK OF PERIOD I

ORGANIZATION

Jesus' gaining a few men as disciples.

WORKS

A demonstration of superhuman knowledge. A miracle on nature. Miracles of healing. A cleansing of the Temple.

RECEPTION

Many Jerusalemites' believing in Jesus, but not very intelligently. A Sanhedrist profoundly moved.

Rejection of Jesus by the Jewish rulers.

TEACHING

Jesus' private announcement of the Messianic Kingdon. A private discourse on Salvation and the Messianic Kingdom.

ANALYSIS OF THE WORK OF PERIOD II

ORGANIZATION

His disciples baptising for Jesus.

WORK

A demonstration of superhuman knowledge.

RECEPTION

Many Judeans baptised. Many Samaritans' believing in Jesus' Christhood and mission.

Persecution of John the Baptist by the Pharisees and Herod Antipas. The Pharisees' menacing Jesus.

TEACHING

Jesus' public announcement of the Messianic Kingdom. A private discourse on Salvation and the Messianic Kingdom.

12

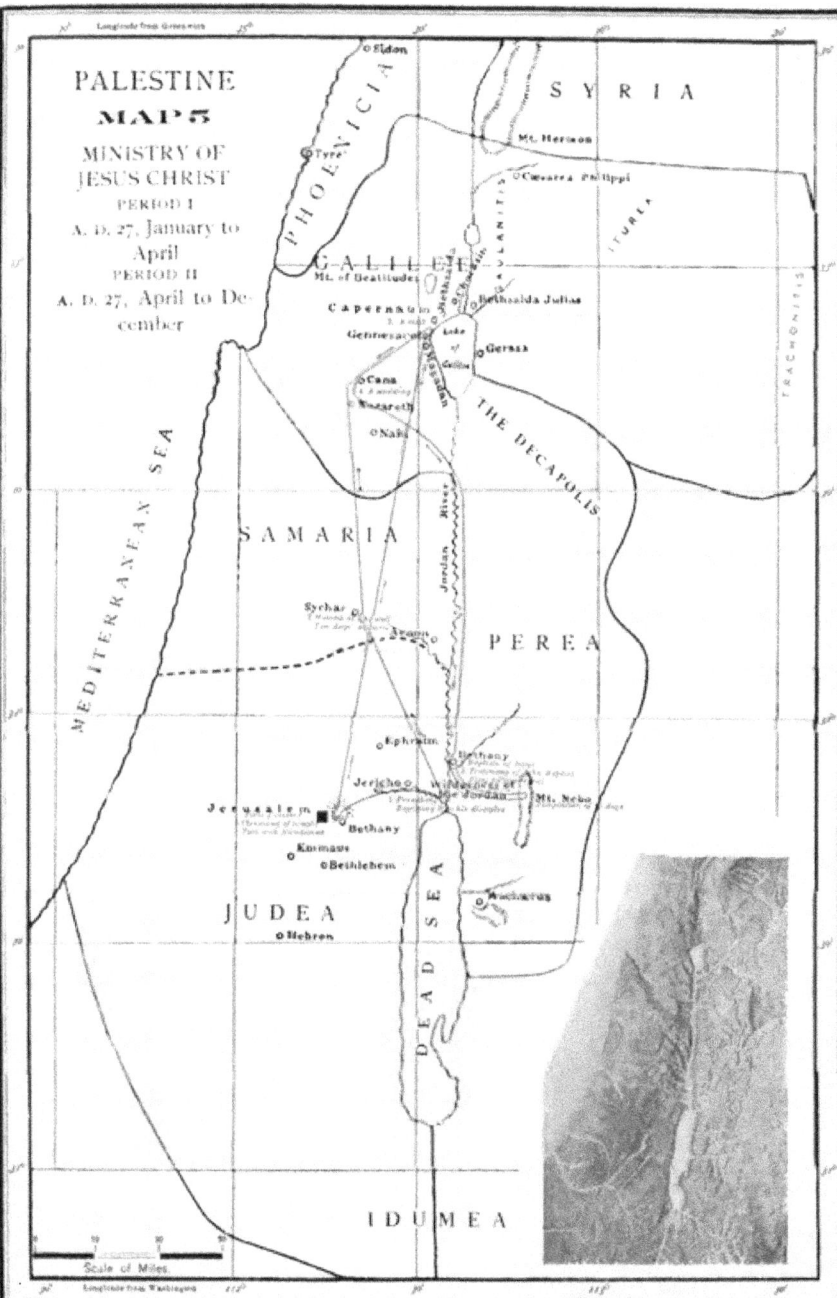

PALESTINE
MAP 5
MINISTRY OF JESUS CHRIST
PERIOD I
A. D. 27, January to April
PERIOD II
A. D. 27, April to December

THE MINISTRY OF JESUS CHRIST

ANALYSIS OF THE WORK OF PERIOD III

ORGANIZATION

Jesus' disciples called upon to leave business for him.

WORKS

A miracle on nature.   Miracles of healing.

RECEPTION

Sought for his miracles by the sick from all adjacent provinces and countries.   Extolled very generally for his teaching.

His great popularity threatening to attract the jealous notice of Herod Antipas.   Jesus' life attempted by his townsmen.   The conspiracy of the Pharisees against Jesus' life, and later of the Herodians with them.   The Pharisees' persecutions of Jesus.

TEACHING

Jesus' public announcement of the Messianic Kingdom. A public discourse on Salvation and the Messianic Kingdom.

14

PALESTINE
MAP 6
MINISTRY OF
JESUS CHRIST
PERIOD III
A. D. 27, 28
December to April

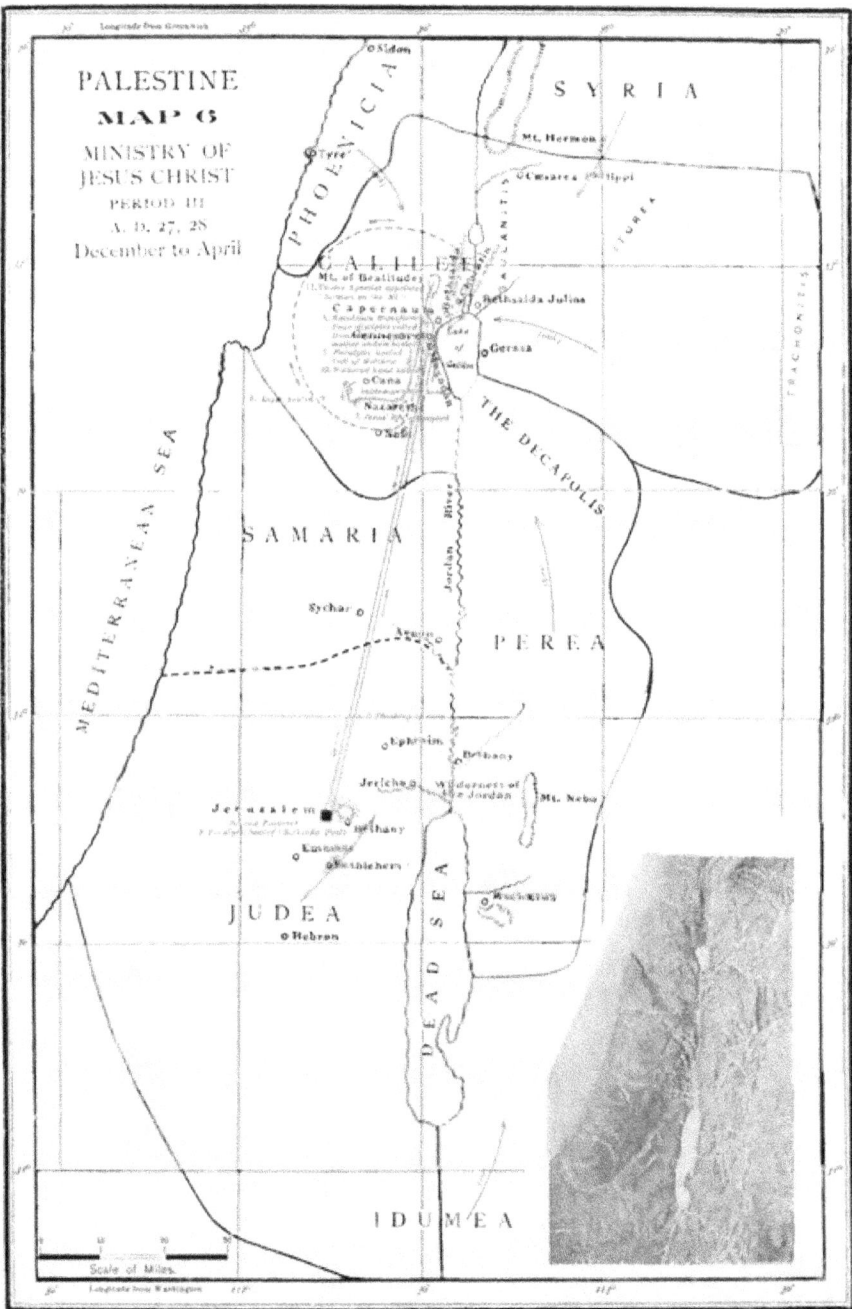

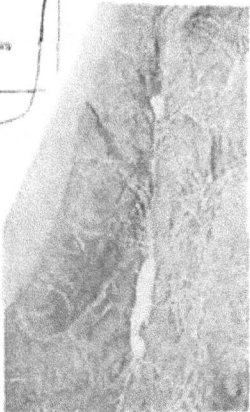

SYRIA

PHOENICIA

Sidon

Tyre

Mt. Hermon

Caesarea Philippi

GAULANITIS

ITUREA

GALILEE

Mt. of Beatitudes

Capernaum

Bethsaida Julias

TRACHONITIS

Lake of

Gerasa

Cana

Nain

Nazareth

THE DECAPOLIS

MEDITERRANEAN SEA

SAMARIA

Sychar

Jordan River

Aenon

PEREA

Ephraim

Bethany

Jericho

Wilderness of the Jordan

Mt. Nebo

Jerusalem

Bethany

Emmaus

Bethlehem

JUDEA

Hebron

DEAD SEA

IDUMEA

Scale of Miles.

THE MINISTRY OF JESUS CHRIST

ORGANIZATION

Jesus selection of Twelve Apostles to accompany him and become his ministers.

WORKS

Miracles of healing. A resurrection.

RECEPTION

Jesus once publicly hailed as Christ. Generally believed to be an old prophet risen from the dead. The doubt of John the Baptist.

The protests of Jesus' family and friends against his ardor. Persecutions of the Pharisees.

TEACHING

A public parabolic discourse on Salvation and the Messianic Kingdom.

PALESTINE
MAP 7
MINISTRY OF
JESUS CHRIST
PERIOD IV
A. D. 28
Summer and Fall

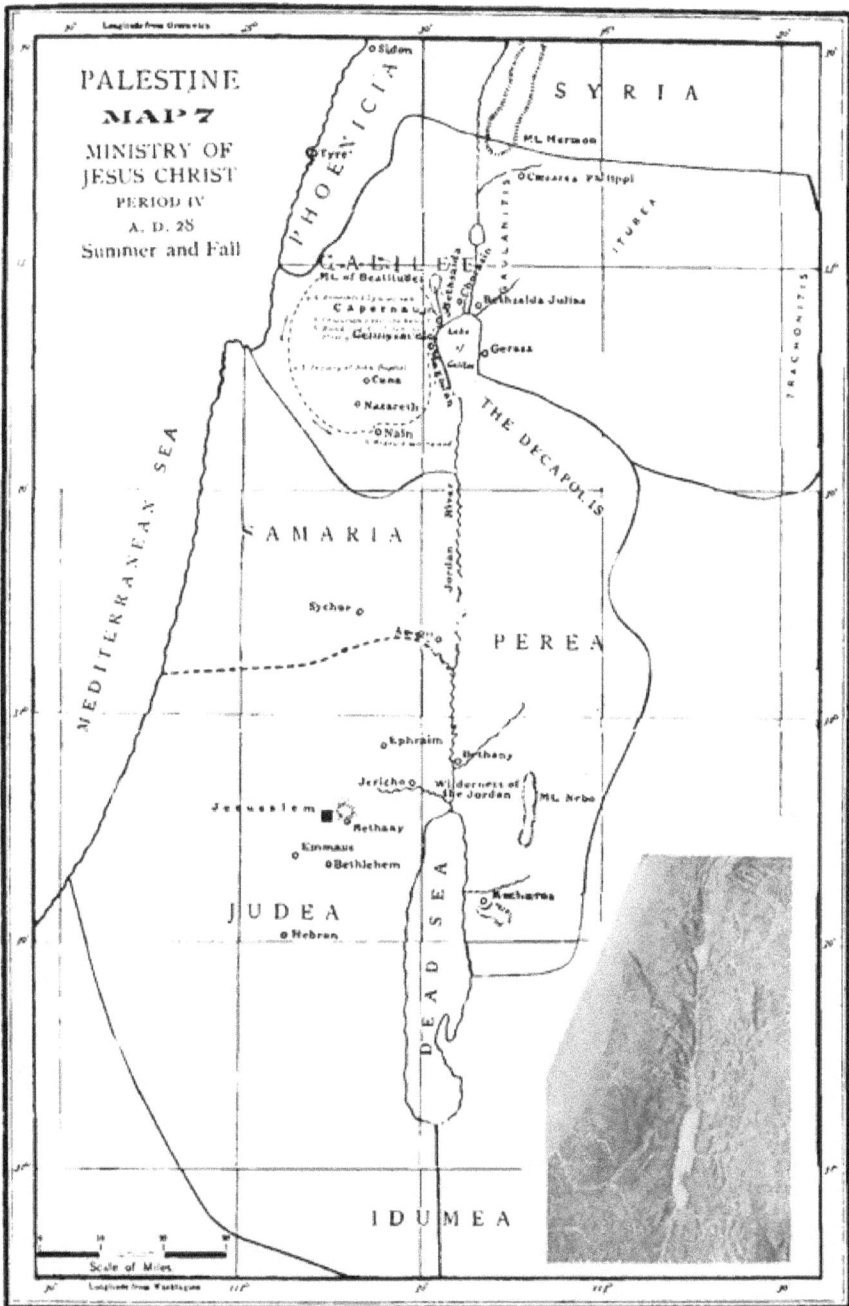

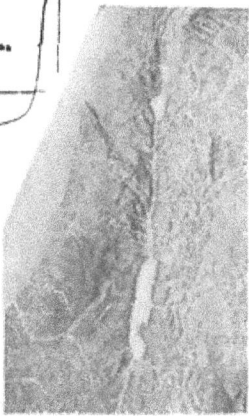

SYRIA

o Sidon

PHOENICIA

Mt. Hermon

o Tyre

o Cæsarea Philippi

ITUREA

GAULANITIS

GALILEE

Mt. of Beatitudes

CAPERNAUM

o Bethsaida Julias

Bethsaida

Lake

o Gerasa

Gennesaret

o Gadara

TRACHONITIS

o Cana

o Nazareth

o Nain

THE DECAPOLIS

MEDITERRANEAN SEA

SAMARIA

Jordan River

Sychar o

Æno o

PEREA

o Ephraim

Bethany

Jericho o

Wilderness of the Jordan

Mt. Nebo

Jerusalem

Bethany

Emmaus o

o Bethlehem

JUDEA

o Hebron

DEAD SEA

Machærus

IDUMEA

Scale of Miles

THE MINISTRY OF JESUS CHRIST.

ANALYSIS OF THE WORK OF PERIOD V

ORGANIZATION

The self-activity of the apostles, in a Jewish mission. Their pairing by Jesus. His selection of three of them as his special confidants.

WORKS

Miracles on nature. Miracles of healing and resurrections, both by Jesus and his apostles.

RECEPTION

Many women among Jesus' disciples. The Galileans' attempting to make Jesus king by force.

Rejected by the Gerasenes. Deserted by the Galileans. Herod Antipas' beheading of John the Baptist, and attempting to find Jesus.

TEACHING

A public discourse on the Essentially Spiritual Character of His Mission.

PALESTINE
MAP 8
MINISTRY OF
JESUS CHRIST
PERIOD V
A. D. 28, 29
Fall to Spring

Longitude from Greenwich

SYRIA

PHOENICIA

Sidon

Tyre

Mt. Hermon

Cæsarea Philippi

GALILEE

GAULANITIS

ITURÆA

Mt. of Beatitudes

Bethsaida Julias

Capernaum

Gennesaret

TRACHONITIS

Gerasa

Cana

Nazareth

Nain

THE DECAPOLIS

MEDITERRANEAN SEA

SAMARIA

Jordan River

PEREA

Sychar

Ænon

Ephraim

Bethany

Jericho

Wilderness of the Jordan

Mt. Nebo

Jerusalem

Bethany

Emmaus

Bethlehem

DEAD SEA

JUDEA

Hebron

Machærus

IDUMEA

Scale of Miles.

Longitude from Washington

THE MINISTRY OF JESUS CHRIST

ANALYSIS OF THE WORK OF PERIOD VI

ORGANIZATION

The apostles' formal acceptance of Jesus as Saviour and Divine Christ.

WORKS

Miracles on nature. Miracles of healing both by Jesus and at least one disciple. Jesus' transfiguration.

RECEPTION

Sought by many Gentiles in all their countries that he visited.

Persecutions of the Pharisees. The Sadducees' uniting with the Pharisees and Herodians in the deadly conspiracy against him. Taunted by his ''brothers.''

TEACHING

Private discourses to the apostles on the Sacrificial Nature of His Mission.

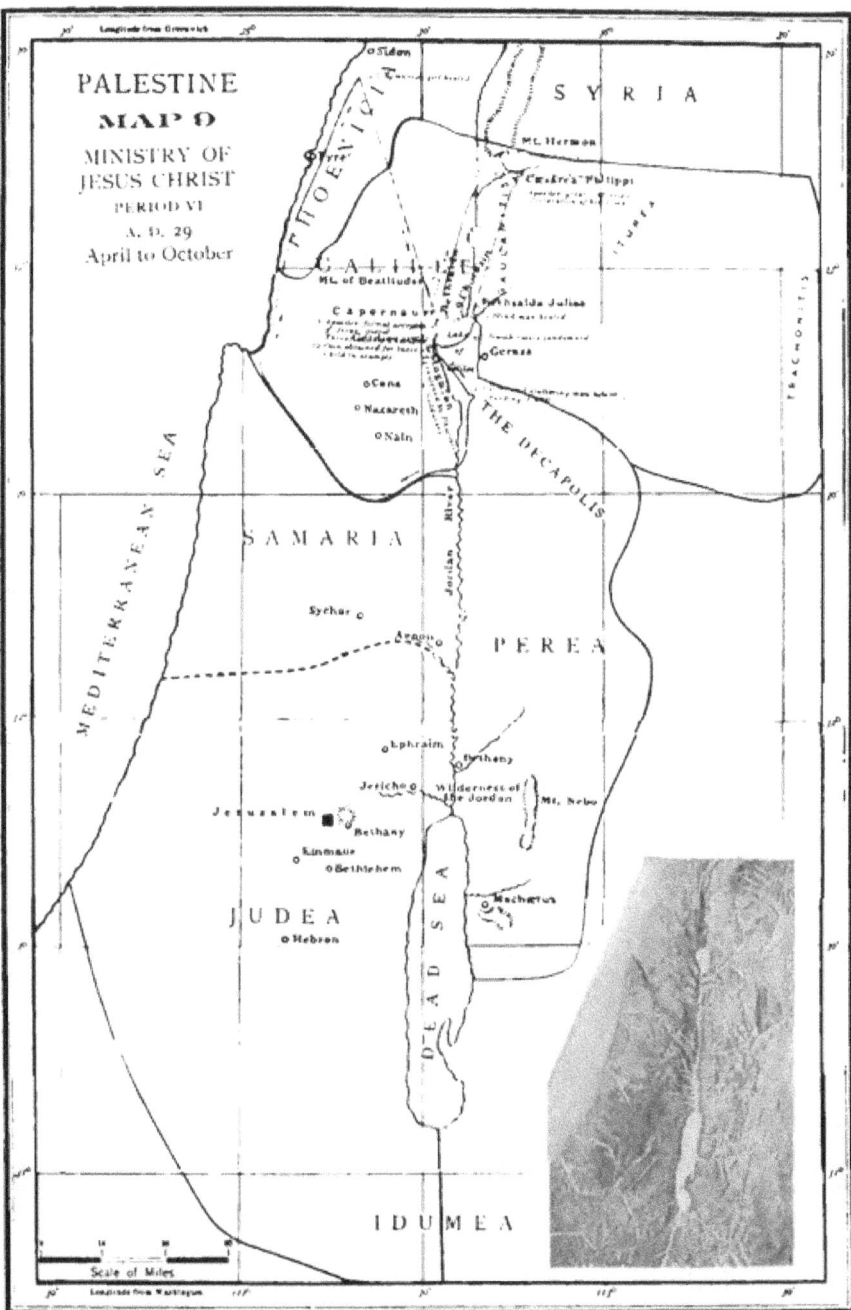

THE MINISTRY OF JESUS CHRIST

ANALYSIS OF THE WORK OF PERIOD VII

ORGANIZATION

Jesus' calling and pairing of seventy more disciples and their self-activity in a mission in Perea.

WORKS

Miracles of healing both by Jesus and his Seventy Disciples.

RECEPTION

Many Pereans' believing in Jesus.

The Jerusalemites' dividing about him.   Persecutions by the Pharisees and and Sanhedrists.   His life twice attempted by the Jerusalemites.

TEACHING

Public claims made in Jerusalem as Saviour and Divine. Public announcement in Perea thro disciples, of the Messianic Kingdom.   Public parabolic discourses on Salvation and the Messianic Kingdom.

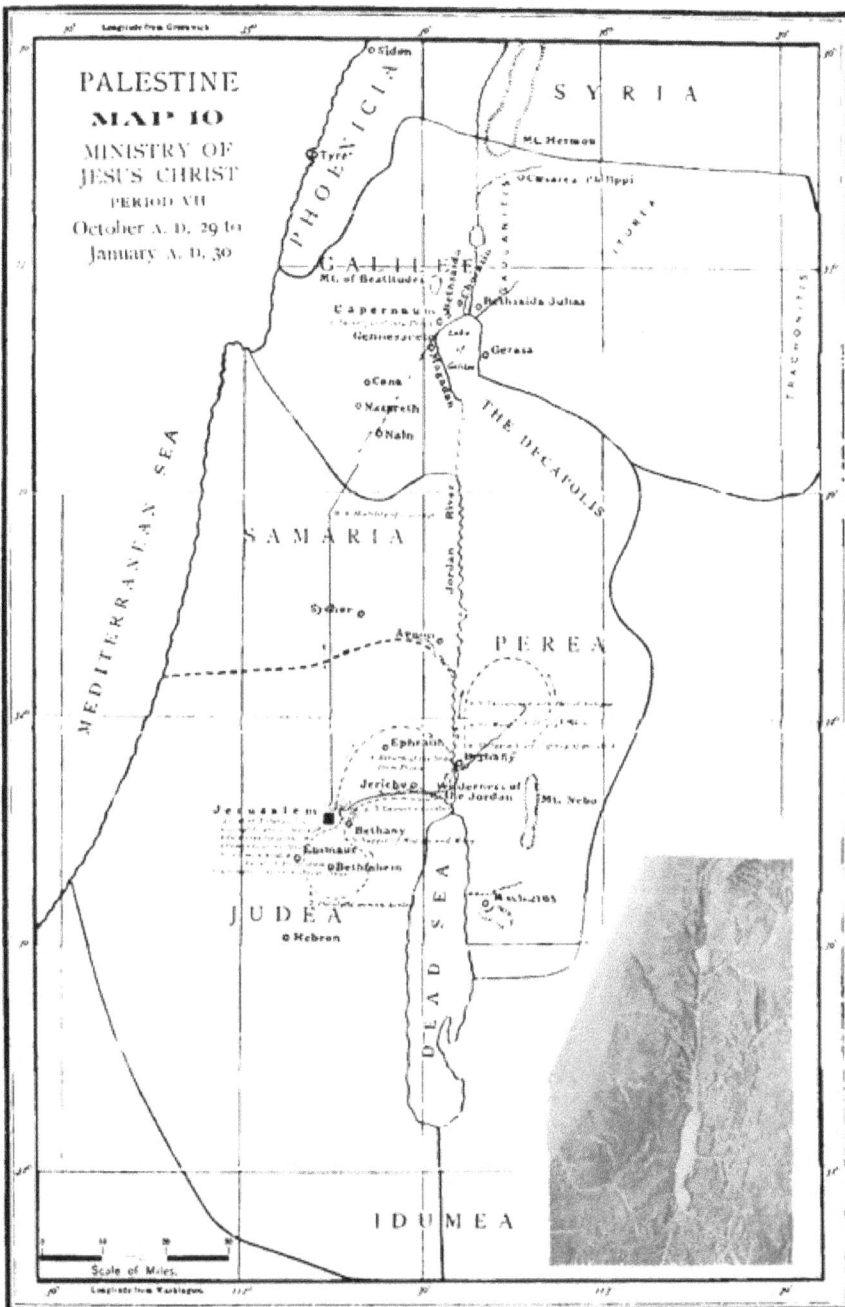

PALESTINE
MAP 10
MINISTRY OF
JESUS CHRIST
PERIOD VII
October A. D. 29 to
January A. D. 30

SYRIA

PHOENICIA

O Sidon

Mt. Hermon

O Tyre

O Cæsarea Philippi

GALILEE

Mt. of Beatitudes

Capernaum

Gennesaret

Bethsaida Julias

Gerasa

O Cana

O Nazareth

O Nain

MEDITERRANEAN SEA

SAMARIA

Jordan River

Sychar O

Ænon

PEREA

THE DECAPOLIS

ITUREA

TRACHONITIS

O Ephraim

Bethany

Jericho O

Wilderness of
the Jordan

Mt. Nebo

Jerusalem

Bethany

Emmaus

O Bethlehem

JUDEA

O Hebron

DEAD SEA

Masada 2165

Scale of Miles.

IDUMEA

THE MINISTRY OF JESUS CHRIST

ANALYSIS OF THE WORK OF PERIOD VIII

ORGANIZATION

The apostles' acceptance of martyrdom to continue to be followers of Jesus.

WORKS

A miracle on nature. Miracles of healing. A resurrection. A royal entry into Jerusalem. A cleansing of the Temple.

RECEPTION

Many Jerusalemites' believing, including some secret disciples in the Sanhedrin. Palestinian pilgrims' at Jerusalem hailing him as Christ and King. The Passover pilgrims', generally, counting him a prophet.

The Sanhedrin's conspiring against his life, and against Lazarus'. The betrayal of Judas. The desertion of the apostles. Jesus arrested and condemned by the Sanhedrin ; and the people's uniting with them in demanding his death. His rejection by Herod Antipas. His crucifixion by Pilate.

TEACHING

Public claim made to Christhood. Final public discourse on Salvation and the Kingdon of a Divine Christ. Private discourses to the apostles on Spiritual Life in His Hingdom.

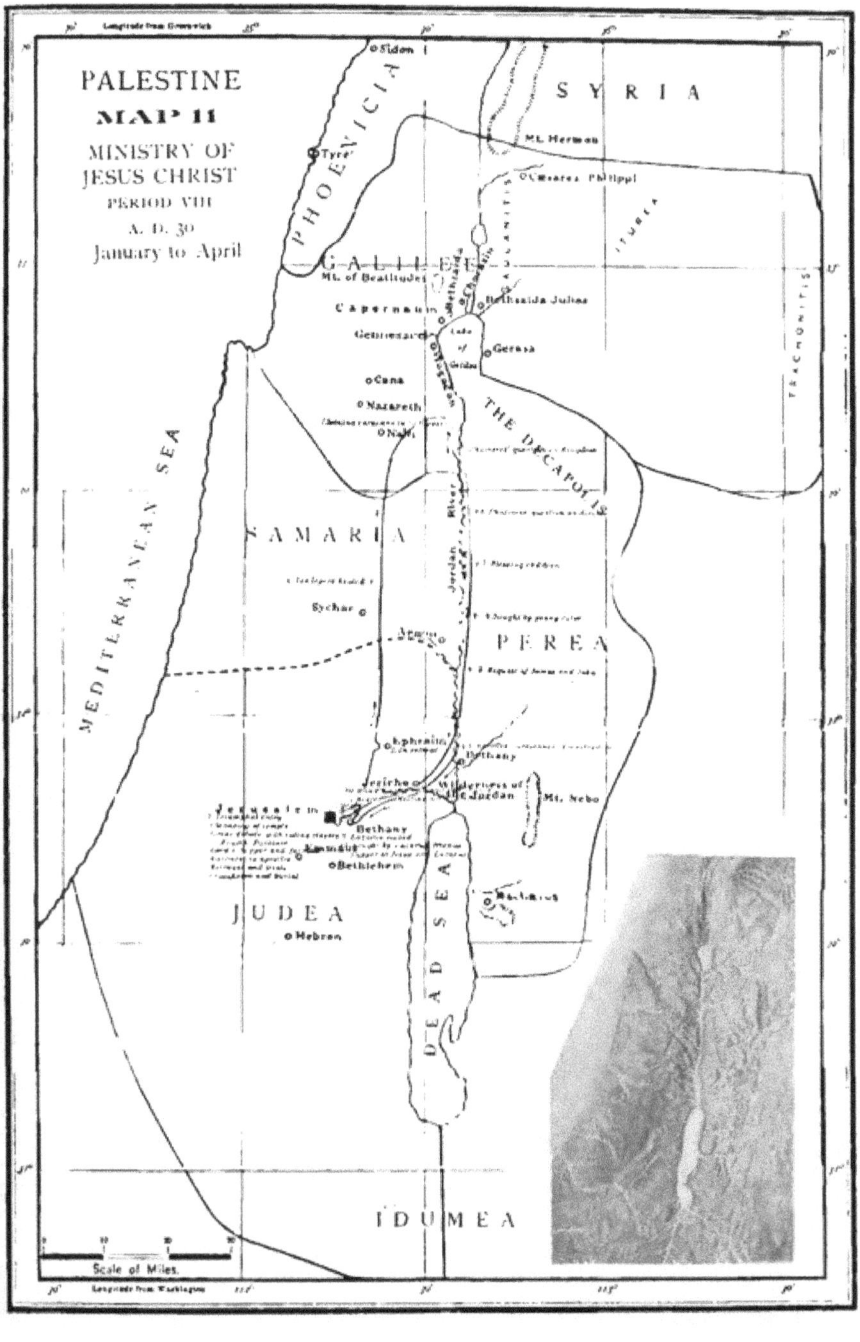

PALESTINE
MAP 11
MINISTRY OF
JESUS CHRIST
PERIOD VIII
A. D. 30
January to April
Sidon
PHOENICIA
Tyre
SYRIA
Mt. Hermon
Caesarea Philippi
ITURAEA
GAULANITIS
TRACHONITIS
GALILEE
Mt. of Beatitudes
Bethsaida Julias
Capernaum
Gennesaret
Gerasa
Cana
Nazareth
Nain
THE DECAPOLIS
SAMARIA
Sychar
Jordan River
PEREA
MEDITERRANEAN SEA
Ephraim
Bethany
Jericho
Wilderness of Judea
Mt. Nebo
Jerusalem
Bethany
Emmaus
Bethlehem
JUDEA
Hebron
DEAD SEA
IDUMEA
Scale of Miles.

NOTE ON MAP 12

The plat of the Temple Area will serve also to supplement maps 2, 3, 5, 6, 10, and 13.

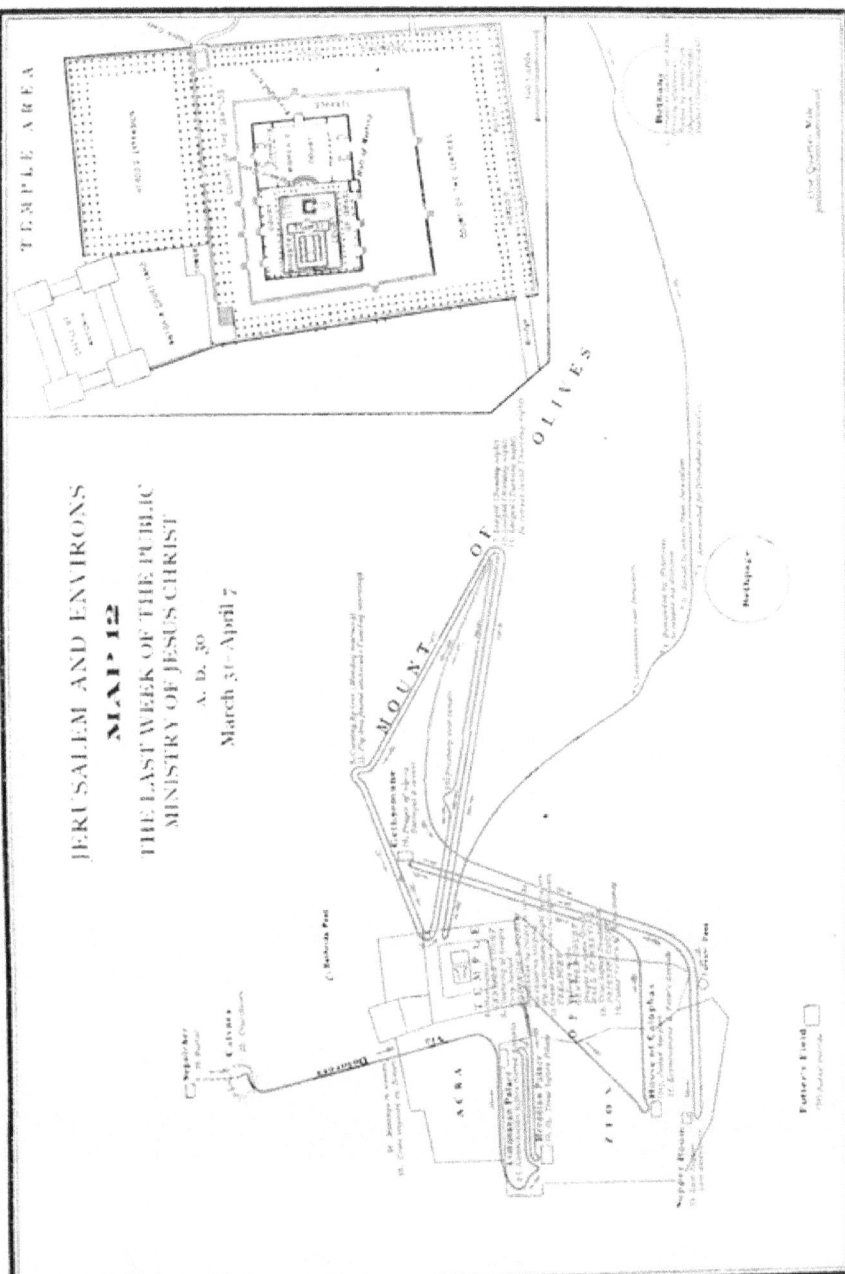

TEMPLE AREA

JERUSALEM AND ENVIRONS

MAP 12

THE LAST WEEK OF THE PUBLIC
MINISTRY OF JESUS CHRIST

A. D. 30

March 31–April 7

MOUNT OF OLIVES

TEMPLE

ACRA

ZION

Potter's Field

THE MINISTRY OF JESUS CHRIST

ANALYSIS OF THE WORK OF PERIOD IX

ORGANIZATION

The apostles and all of his disciples commissioned by Jesus to evangelize the world.

WORKS

Jesus' resurrection. His appearances and disappearances. A miracle on nature. His ascension.

RECEPTION

The final and complete conviction of the apostles and more than five hundred other disciples that Jesus was the Christ.

The conspiracy of the Sanhedrists against the evidence of Jesus' resurrection.

TEACHING

Private discourses to apostles and other disciples on Salvation and the World Wide Consumation of His Kingdom.

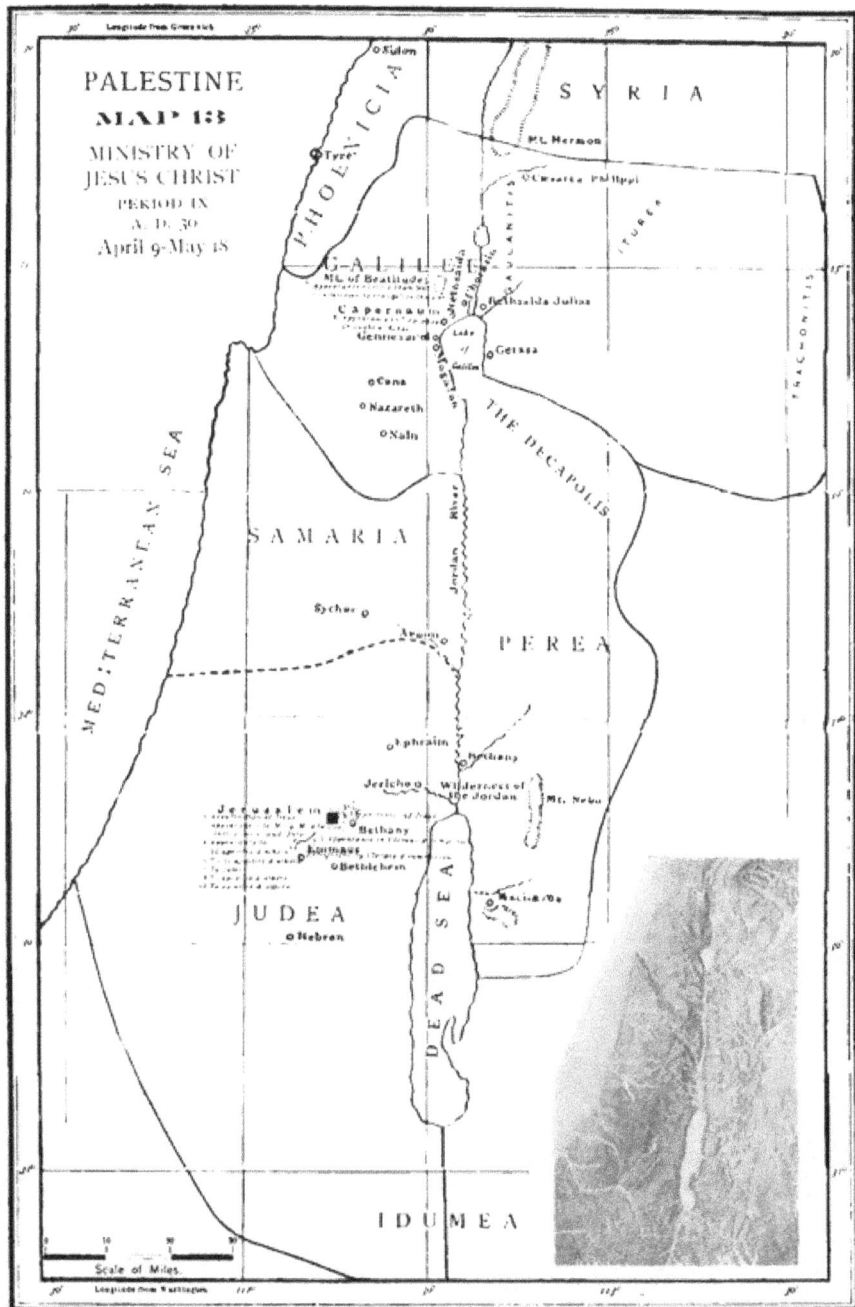

PALESTINE
MAP 13
MINISTRY OF
JESUS CHRIST
PERIOD IX
A. D. 30
April 9-May 18

Longitude from Greenwich

SYRIA

PHOENICIA

o Sidon

o Tyre

Mt. Hermon

o Cæsarea Philippi

GALILEE

ITUREA

Mt. of Beatitudes

Capernaum

Gennesaret

Lake of Galilee

Gerasa

AURANITIS

Bethsaida Julias

TRACHONITIS

o Cana

o Nazareth

o Nain

THE DECAPOLIS

MEDITERRANEAN SEA

SAMARIA

Jordan River

Sychar o

Ænon o

PEREA

o Ephraim

Bethany

Jericho o

Wilderness of
the Jordan

Mt. Nebo

Jerusalem

Bethany

Emmaus

o Bethlehem

DEAD SEA

JUDEA

o Hebron

IDUMEA

Scale of Miles.

Longitude from Washington

ERRATA

On Map 3, for " Rabis " should be the word rabbis.

On page 32, in the second line under " Period III," for " 7 a. m." should be 7 p. m.

On page 32, on the fifth line from the bottom, following the word "Preaching," the words should be inserted—Healing of a demoniac.

On page 36, on the fourth line, for " Perea " should be Judea.

On page 39, in the sixth line, for " Map " should be the word Maps ; and in the tenth line of the same page, for "appearance " should be the word appearances.

CHRONOLOGICAL TABLE

THE CHILDHOOD AND YOUTH OF JESUS CHRIST.

Maps 1, 2, 3, 4.

B. C.		Jerusalem.
6.	October.	Annunciation to Zacharias.
		Hebron.
6-5.	Oct. to Mar.	Elizabeth in retirement.
		Nazareth.
5.	March.	Annunciation to Mary.
		Hebron.
	April to June.	Mary's visit to Elizabeth.
	June.	Birth of John the Baptist.
		Nazareth.
		Annunciation to Joseph. His marriage with Mary.
		Bethlehem.
	December 25.	Inn Stable. Birth of Jesus Christ. Vision and adoration of the shepherds.
4.	January 1.	Circumcision of Jesus.
		Jerusalem.
	About Feb. 2.	Temple. Presentation of Jesus.
	·	Bethlehem.
	February.	Adoration of the Magi. Flight into Egypt. The slaying of the infants.
		Egypt.
	May.	Return to Palestine and Nazareth.
A. D.		Jerusalem.
8.	April 8-15.	Earliest Passover Feast. Discussion with the rabbis. Return to Nazareth.
		Jordan Wilderness.
26.	June.	Appearance of John the Baptist.

THE MINISTRY OF JESUS CHRIST.

PERIOD I. Map 5.

		Bethany, Perea.
27.	January.	Baptism of Jesus.

A. D.

Mt. Nebo.

Jan. & Feb.   Forty Days.   Temptation of Jesus.

Bethany, Perea.

February.   Fortieth Day.   Deputation of Sanhedrists to John the
                Baptist.
Next Day.   Jesus' Coming
Next Two Days.   Jesus' making disciples.

Cana.

Three Days Later.   House.   Jesus at a wedding.
Seven Days Later.   Same House.   Miracle of water
      and wine.

Capernaum.

Mar. - Apr.   Later.   Jesus and family and disciples on a visit.

Jerusalem.

April 11-18.   First Passover Feast.
             Temple.   Driving out traders.
A Night.   Dialogue with Nicodemus.

PERIOD II.   MAP 5.

Judea.

Apr. to Dec.   Later.   Jesus' preaching and baptizing.

Aenon.

December.   John the Baptist's arrest by Herod Antipas.

Sychar.

One Day.   Jacob's Well.   Jesus' dialogue with a wo-
      man.
Next Two Days.   Preaching.

PERIOD III.   Maps 6, 12.

Cana.

Later.   7 a.m.   Healing of a courtier's son.

Nazareth.

27-28. Winter.   Sabbath.   Synagogue.   Jesus' sermon.
             Attempt of townsmen to kill him.

Capernaum.

Later.   Lake Shore.   Boat.   Preaching.
             Second call of the first disciples.
Sabbath.   Synagogue.   Preaching.
             Afternoon and Evening.   Peter's House.
             Healing of many.

A Desert Place.

Next Day.   Withdrawal and prayer.

32

Galilee.

Later. First Tour. Healing of a leper.

Capernaum.

28. Winter
or Spring.

Home of Jesus. Preaching. Healing of a paralytic.
Lake Shore. Preaching.
Place of Toll. Call of Matthew.

Jerusalem.

Mar. 30-Apr. 5

Second Passover Feast.
Sabbath. Bethesda Pool. Healing of a paralytic.
Later. Temple. Teaching. Conspiracy of Pharisees against Jesus' life.

Judea.

April.

Next Sabbath. Plucking corn.

Capernaum.

Next Sabbath. Synagogue. Healing of a withered hand. Herodians join in the conspiracy of the Pharisees.
Later. Lake Shore. Healings. Preaching.

Mt. Beatitude.

A Night. Selection of Twelve Apostles.
Next Day. Healings. Sermon on the Kingdom.

PERIOD IV. Map 7.

Capernaum.

Later. Healing of a centurion's servant.

Nain.

Summer.

Raising of a widow's son to life.

Galilee.

Message from John the Baptist.
House of Simon the Pharisee. Annointing by a woman.

Autumn.

Completion of Second Tour of Galilee.

Capernaum.

One Day. Home of Jesus. Preaching. Healing of a blind and dumb demoniac.
Lake Shore. First Great Group of Parables on the Kingdom, the Sower, the Candle, the Seed, the Tares, the Mustard Seed, the Leaven, the Hid Treasure, the Pearl of Price, the Net.

PERIOD V. Map 8.

Lake Galilee.

Same Day. Boat. Storm stilled.

33

A. D.

Gerasa.

Next Day. Healing of two demoniacs.

Capernaum.

Next Day. Matthew's House. A feast.
Healing of a woman with flux.
Jairus' House. Raising of his daughter to life.
Healing of two blind men. Healing of a dumb
demoniac.

Nazareth.

28-29. Winter.   Sabbath. Synagogue. Preaching. Again rejected.

Galilee.

Later. Third Tour. Sending out the Twelve, two by
two, thro Galilee.

Capernaum.

29. April.   News of John the Baptist's death of the month
before in Machaerus.

Bethsaida Julias.

One Day. A Desert Place. Feeding of five thousand.
Attempt to crown Jesus king.

Lake Galilee.

Next Day. 3-6 a. m. Walking on the water.

Plain of Gennesaret.

Same Day. Cities and villages. Healing of many.

Capernaum.

Next Day. Synagogue. Discourse on Spiritual Food.
Desertion of Galileans.

PERIOD VI. Map 9.

Capernaum.

Same day. Fidelity of the apostles.
Pharisees offended.

17-24   Third Passover Feast. Unattended by Jesus
on account of the deadly hostility of Pharisees
and Herodians.

Phoenicia.

Summer.   Healing of a demoniac girl.

Decapolis.

Healing of a deaf and stuttering man.
Mountain on Lake Shore. Feeding of four
thousand.

Magadan.

One Day. Sadducees found in the conspiracy of Pharisees and Herodians.

34

Lake Galilee.

Same Day. Boat. Jesus' denunciation of the rulers' expectations of a kingdom.

Bethsaida Julias.

Later. Healing a blind man.

Base of Mt. Hermon.

Later. First full confession of apostles of Jesus' divinity and Christhood. Jesus' first formal prediction to apostles of his death and resurrection.

Mt. Hermon.

Six Days Later. Transfiguration.

Base of Mt. Hermon.

Next Day. Healing of a demoniac boy.

Galilee.

Autumn. Secret Journey. Jesus' second formal prediction to apostles of his death and resurrection. Quarrel of apostles.

Capernaum.

Tax coin obtained. Two procrastinating volunteers. Taunt of Jesus' "brothers."

PERIOD VII. Maps 10, 12.

Capernaum.

October. Seventy disciples sent out two by two into Perea.

Samaria.

Inhospitality of a village.

Jerusalem.

11-18. Feast of Tabernacles.
15. Temple. Arrival of Jesus.
16. Teaching.
17. Sanhedrists' attempt to arrest him.

Mt. Olives.

Night. Lodging.

Jerusalem.

18. Temple. Adulteress brought before Jesus.
His declaration of divinity.
Jerusalemites' attempt to kill him.
Healing of a blind man.
The man ex-communicated.
His confession of Jesus.
Parable of the Good Shepherd.

A. D.   Judea.

November.   Return of the Seventy. Question of a lawyer, and parable of the Good Samaritan.

Bethany, Perea.

House. Martha's entertainment, and reproach.

Judea.

Nov. or Dec.   Model of prayer. Parable of the Friend at Midnight.

House of a Pharisee. Denunciation of Pharisees and lawyers.

Parables of the Foolish Rich Man, the Wedding Feast, the Wise Steward, the Barren Fig Tree.

Sabbath Day. Synagogue. Healing of a paralytic woman.

Jerusalem.

Dec. 20-27.   Feast of Dedication.

Temple. Attempts to stone and to arrest Jesus.

Perea.

Later. Threatened by Pharisees with Herod Antipas.

30.   January.   Sabbath. House of a Pharisee. Healing of a man of dropsy. Parable of the Great Supper.

Later. Second Great Group of Parables on the Kingdom: the Building a Tower, the King Making War, the Lost Sheep, the Lost Coin, the Lost Son, the Unjust Steward, the Rich Man and Lazarus, the Unprofitable Servants.

PERIOD VIII. Maps 11, 12.

Perea.

One Day. Summons to Bethany, Judea.

Two Days Later. Early morning. The apostles' acceptance of martyrdom.

Bethany, Judea.

Same Day. Evening. Raising of Lazarus to life.

Jerusalem.

Later. Sanhedrists determine on the death of Jesus.

Ephraim.

Feb. to Mar.   Jesus' retirement with apostles.

Samaria.

March.   Healing of ten lepers.

36

A. D.   Galilee.
                              Pharisees' question on the Kingdom.
                              Parables of the Importunate Widow, and the
                              Pharisee and the Publican.

                              Perea.
                              Questions on divorce and celibacy. Blessing
                                of children.
                  A sunset. Without a City Gate. Young ruler's ques-
                              tion; parable of the Laborers in the Vineyard.
                  Later. Jesus' third formal prediction to apostles of his
                              death and resurrection. Request of James and
                              John.

                              Jericho.
      30. Thursday. Healing of blind Bartimaeus and compan-
                         ion.
                      Home of Zacchaeus. Lodging.
      31. Friday.   Zachaeus' public profes-
                                              sion of conversion.
                              Parable of the Pounds.

                              Bethany, Judea.
                              House of Simon. Arrival.
Apr. 1. Saturday.   Visited by Lazarus' friends
                                              from Jerusalem.
                      Evening.   A supper and Judas' anger.

                              Jerusalem.
                              A price already put by Sanhedrists on infor-
                              mation for Jesus' arrest; and their determining
                              on the death of Lazarus.

                              Mt. Olives.
      2. Sunday. Triumphal entry into Jerusalem.
      3. Monday. Early Morning. Cursing a fig-tree.

                              Jerusalem.
                      Temple. Driving out traders. Singing of
                                 children.

                              Mt. Olives.
      4. Tuesday. Early Morning. Blight of fig-tree. Lesson.

                              Jerusalem.
                      Temple. Great Debate with the Ruling
                                 Classes, with parables of the Two
                                 Sons, the Wicked Husbandmen,
                                 the Marriage of the King's Son. A
                                 widow's mites. Sought by Greeks.
                                 Jesus' last appeal.

                              Mt. Olives.
                      Sunset. Prediction of the Last Things, with
                                 parables, of the Fig Tree and all the
                                 Trees, the Householder, the Talents,
                                 the Sheep and the Goats.

                              37

Mt. Olives.

Night. Jesus' fourth formal prediction to
apostles of his death and resurrection.

5. Wednesday. Retirement.

Jerusalem.

Afternoon. Judas' purchasing the materials of
the Pascal Supper.
House of Caiphas. Sanhedrists'
determining on the arrest of Jesus
after the Passover; entrance of
Judas, his bargain to betray him.

Mt. Olives.

6. Thursday. Fourth Passover. Peter and John's going
to prepare the Pascal Supper.

Jerusalem.

6-11 p. m. House of a Disciple. Pascal Supper, with discharge of Judas, predictions of denials and desertion, and Farewell Discourse.

Mt. Olives.

Farewell Discourse concluded and prayer.

7. Friday. Gethsemane. Midnight. Prayer of agony.
1 a. m. Betrayal: healing of
Malchus' ear.; desertion of
apostles; arrest of Jesus.

Jerusalem.

2-3 a. m. House of Caiaphas. Ecclesiastical
examinations: First, before Annas, Second,
before Caiaphas; Third, before the Sanhedrists; Peter's three denials and remorse.
3-5 a. m. House of Caiaphas. Mockery and
abuse.
5 a. m. Temple. Ecclesiastical trial and conviction of blasphemy. Re-
morse of Judas.
5-6 a. m. Potter's Field. Suicide of Judas.
Herodian Palace. Civil trial before
Pilate.
Asmonaean Palace. Civil exami-
nation before Herod Antipas; mockery.
6-7 a. m. Herodian Palace. Civil trial concluded with scourging, mockery and abuse, and
Pilate's sentence of Jesus to crucifixion.

Calvary.

9 a. m.-12 m. Crucifixion. Jesus provision for
Mary. Reviled by his enemies.
Penitence of one malefactor.
12 m-3 p. m. Darkness.
3 p. m. Jesus' last four sayings on the cross.
His death. Earthquake.

38

Joseph's Garden.

3-6 p. m. Body taken down and buried by Joseph in his own sepulcher.

8. Saturday. A guard of Roman soldiers set by the Sanhedrists at the sepulcher.

Period IX. Map 12, 13.

9. Sunday. Sunrise. Resurrection of Jesus. Tomb visited by women friends. Mary Magdalene's bringing John and Peter. Jesus' appearance to Mary Magdalene, and the other women.

Jerusalem.

Afternoon. Appearance to Peter.

Emmaus.

Afternoon and Evening. Appearance to Cleopas and a companion.

Jerusalem.

Evening. House of a Disciple. Appearance to ten apostles and other disciples.

16. Sunday. House of a Disciple. Appearance to the Eleven apostles and other disciples.

Capernaum.

A sunrise. Appearance to seven apostles.

A Mt. in Galilee.

Apr. or May. Appearance to apostles and more than five hundred other disciples. Commission to apostles and disciples to evangelize the world.

Jerusalem.

May. Appearance to James-the-Just.

14. Sunday. Appearance to the apostles and other disciples. Commission, and the promise of the Holy Spirit.

18. Thursday. Appearance to apostles and other disciples.

Mt. Olives.

Jesus' leading the same company from Jerusalem. His ascending out of view, with the promise of a second coming.

www.ingramcontent.com/pod-product-compliance
Lightning Source LLC
Chambersburg PA
CBHW021431090426
42739CB00009B/1451